The Many Lives of
Pusheen the Cat

Also by Claire Belton

I Am Pusheen the Cat

Pusheen Coloring Book

Mini Pusheen Coloring Book

Let's Bake!: A Pusheen Cookbook

The Many Lives of
Pusheen the Cat

Claire Belton

Gallery Books

New York   London   Toronto   Sydney   New Delhi

Gallery Books
An Imprint of Simon & Schuster, Inc.
1230 Avenue of the Americas
New York, NY 10020

First Gallery Books trade paperback edition March 2021

GALLERY BOOKS and colophon are registered trademarks of Simon & Schuster, Inc.

For information about special discounts for bulk purchases, please contact Simon &
Schuster Special Sales at 1-866-506-1949 or business@simonandschuster.com.

The Simon & Schuster Speakers Bureau can bring authors to your live event. For
more information or to book an event, contact the Simon & Schuster Speakers
Bureau at 1-866-248-3049 or visit our website at www.simonspeakers.com.

Interior design by Jaime Putorti

Manufactured in the United States of America

7 9 10 8 6

Library of Congress Cataloging-in-Publication Data
Names: Belton, Claire, author.
Title: The many lives of Pusheen the cat / Claire Belton.
Description: First Gallery Books trade paperback edition. | New York :
Gallery Books, 2021.
Identifiers: LCCN 2020049516 (print) | LCCN 2020049517 (ebook) |
ISBN 9781982165390 (paperback) | ISBN 9781982165406 (ebook)
Subjects: LCSH: Cats—Humor. | Cats—Caricatures and cartoons. |
Wit and humor, Pictorial.
Classification: LCC PN6231.C23 B45 2013 (print) | LCC PN6231.C23 (ebook) |
DDC 741.5/6—dc23
LC record available at https://lccn.loc.gov/2020049516
LC ebook record available at https://lccn.loc.gov/2020049517

ISBN 978-1-9821-6539-0
ISBN 978-1-9821-6540-6 (ebook)

For Sarah and Jake

Contents

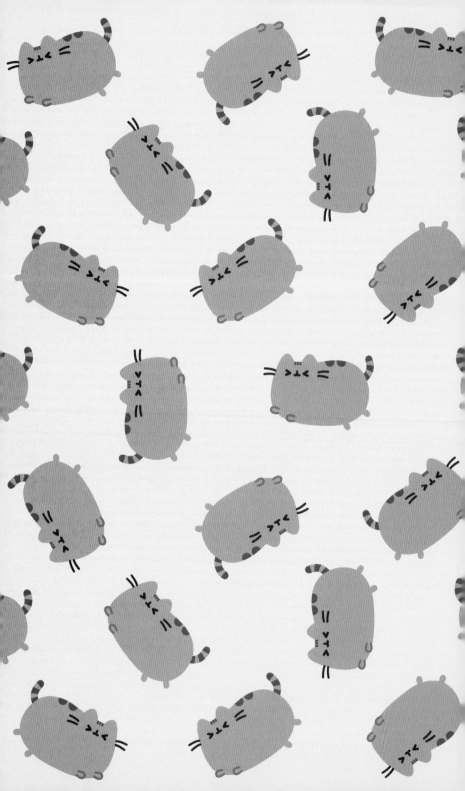

Pusheen

GENDER: Girl

BIRTHDAY: February 18

BEST FEATURE: Toes that look like beans

FAVORITE FOOD: All of them

FAVORITE COLOR: Cream

HOBBIES: Snacking, sleeping, blogging

ATTRIBUTES: Sweet, curious, lazy

Types of Cat Tails

The noodle

The duster

The pine tree

The bottle brush

The question mark

The warning

Events Suitable for Cats

Live music

Parades

Theater

Fine dining

Tips for Sleeping Well

Cozy up your area

Get relaxed

Have a nice bath

Keep a routine

Patterns That Cats Like

Tiger print

Leopard print

Snow leopard print

Cheetah print

Ikat

~~Houndstooth~~

A Study of Toe Beans

Beans

Bean sprouts

Broad beans

String beans

Adulting Essentials

Meal planning

Commuting

Making dough

Getting bread

How to Be a Good Roommate

Help with the laundry

Keep things tidy

Keep a low profile

Respect their privacy

Catfé Drinks

Iced catpusheeno

Meowchiato

Affocato

Espurresso

How to Make Purrfect Coffee

Gather your tools

Use quality beans

Pour nice and slow

Serve with snacks

Where to Find Your Cat

1. Under the table

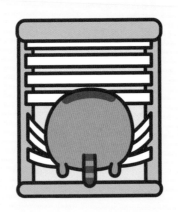

2. Behind the blinds

3. Inside the (empty) tub

4. In your business

Reasons I Love Summer

Camping

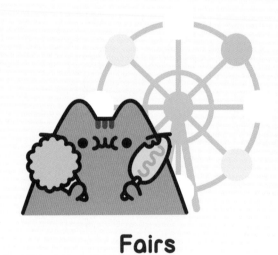

Fairs

Water parks

Air-conditioning

Nicknames for Your Cat

Bun

Roll

Loaf

Food made of flour, water, and yeast or another leavening agent mixed together and baked

How to Have a
Perfect Birthday

Wake up

Eat up

Level up

~~Grow up~~

Pusheen's Guide to
Relaxing

Wear a fuzzy robe

Have a hot drink

Put on comfy slippers

So. Relaxed.

The Scents of Fall

Crunchy leaves

Cozy fires

Ripe apples

Despair

~~Early snow~~

Halloween Activities
for Your Cat

Dress up spooky

Do some tricks

Eat some treats

Play with wrappers

Pusheen's Guide
to Cakes

Cupcake

Birthday cake

Pancake

Patty-cake

Traveling

with Pusheen the Cat

Expectation

Reality

Expectation

Reality

Expectation

Reality

I kinda like you

Pusheen's Guide to
Household Chores

Do the laundry

Wash the dishes

Dust the shelves

~~Vacuum~~

How to Play Baseball

Make the most of left field

Catch what's important

Load the bases

Steal home

Pusheen's Guide to a Balanced Diet

1. Sweet snacks

2. Salty snacks

3. Sweet snacks

4. Salty snacks

Today's Menu

Breakfast:
waffles

Lunch:
sandwiches

Dinner:
frozen food

6 Reasons to Be Thankful for Your Cat

Warms your heart

Warms your seat

Cuddle buddy

Alarm clock buddy

Beautiful friend

Beautiful paperweight

How to Make a Muffin

1. You will need a bowl

2. Get in that bowl

3. Nice work

Pool Party Essentials

Shades

Shades

Wings

Wings

A float

A float

Places I Sat Yesterday

7 a.m.: a chair

12 p.m.: a floor

5 p.m.: a desk

10 p.m.: a bed

Learning to Speak Cat:
Essential Phrases

Nah

Nuh-uh

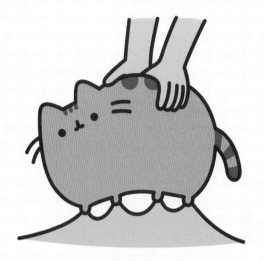

Nope

Absolutely not

Dinner: A How-To

Yell

Shout

Whine

Dine!

Gaming for Cats

Expectation

Reality

Expectation

Reality

Expectation

Reality

Pusheen's
Guide to Houseplants

Water regularly

But not too much

Provide lots of sun

But not too bright

Faux is fine

Proper Dining Etiquette (for Your Cat)

Greet your server

Order your meal

Receive your meal

Send it back

Complex Cat Emotions

Hangry
(hungry + angry)

Borky
(bored + frisky)

Pleepy
(pleased + sleepy)

Fundignified
(fun + undignified)

Social Media for Cats

Twitter

TikTok

Facebook

Instagram

Where to Find a Snack

In a drawer

In a jar

In a bag

In a mirror

Physics with Your Cat

Magnetic energy

Thermal energy

Kinetic energy

Pusheenicorn

GENDER: Girl

BIRTHDAY: February 18

BEST FEATURE: Beautiful hair

FAVORITE FOOD: Cupcakes

FAVORITE COLOR: Pink

HOBBIES: Self-care, adventuring, grazing

ATTRIBUTES: Mysterious, sensitive, caring

How to Tell If Your Cat Is a Unicorn

They are mysterious

They move gracefully

They are very beautiful

They are hard to find

Pusheenicorn's Guide to Disguises

Wear a party hat

Wear a princess hat

Wear a wizard hat

Wear an ice-cream cone

Pusheenicorn:
The Legend

Beautiful

Mysterious

Magical

Sensitive

Fierce

Essential Unicorn Skills

Galloping

Sparkling

Relaxing

Grazing

Pusheenicorn's Motivational Tips

Accept challenges

Overcome obstacles

If things get hard . . .

you can ask for help!

Pusheenicorn's
BEAUTY TIPS

**Admire your beauty
in a clear pool**

**Ponder your beauty
in a pure crystal**

Gaze upon your beauty
in a silver dish

Accept your beauty
in your heart

Pusheenicorn's Horn Tips

Use it to store snacks

Use it for ring toss

Use it for bug repellent

Use it for fashion

Super Pusheenicorn

GENDER: Girl

BIRTHDAY: February 18

BEST FEATURE: Tiny but powerful wings

FAVORITE FOOD: Cookies

FAVORITE COLOR: Purple

HOBBIES: Flying, stargazing, self-expression

ATTRIBUTES: Magical, positive, energetic

Pawsitive Affirmations
with Super Pusheenicorn

Shoot for the stars

Be open to possibilities

Reach your full potential

Happiness Essentials

with Super Pusheenicorn

Practice acceptance

Live in the moment

Spread kindness

Be thankful

Mermaid Pusheen

GENDER: Girl

BIRTHDAY: February 18

BEST FEATURE: Hair accessories

FAVORITE FOOD: Madeleines

FAVORITE COLOR: Aqua

HOBBIES: Swimming & watching beauty tutorials

ATTRIBUTES: Glamorous, fashionable, sassy

How to Tell If Your Cat Is a Mermaid

Likes to play with water

Loves fish

Is a total diva

Rules of the Sea

Make waves

Go with the flow

Fish are friends

Beware of sharks

How to Get
Mermaid Hair

Shampoo well

Rinse well

Apply seaweed mask

Nice work!

Treasure Hunting 101

Go exploring

Find the spot

Start digging

Success!

Mermaid Pusheen

Curious

Glamorous

Fashionable

Bold

The 4 Types of Mermaid Cats

Meowmaids

Purrmaids

Catfish

Bobcats

What's Your Swimming Style?

Backstroke

Freestyle

Butterfly

Doggy paddle

Pusheenosaurus
& Dinosheens

GENDER: Girl

BIRTHDAY: February 18

BEST FEATURE: Very tall

FAVORITE FOOD: Greens

FAVORITE COLOR: Mint

HOBBIES: Stomping around & swinging her tail

ATTRIBUTES: Strong, friendly, always hungry

How to Tell If Your Cat Is a Dinosaur

They have big claws

They have a big appetite

They're just big

Dinosheens' Survival Guide

Run fast

Fly fast

Swim fast

Breakfast

PUSHEENOSAURUS

Strong

Curious

Friendly

Hungry

VERY HUNGRY

Tea rex

How to Care for
Your Pet Dinosheen

Feed them

Play with them

Brush them

Love them

Exercise them

~~Trim their nails~~

What the T. rex May Have Looked Like

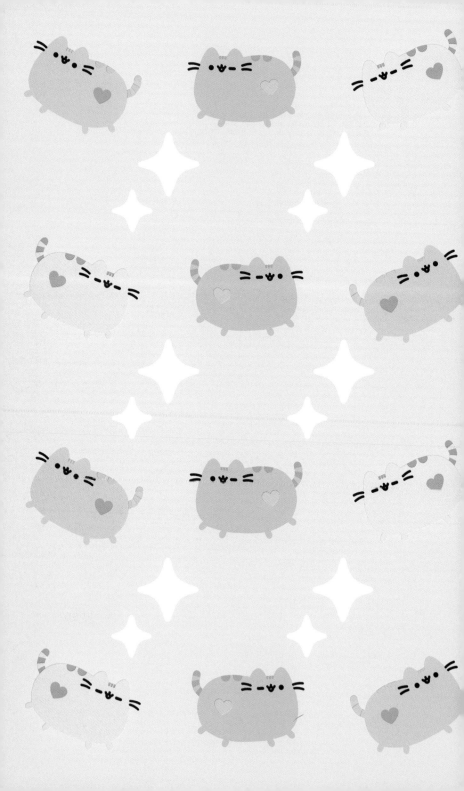

Pastel Pusheens

GENDER: Girls

BIRTHDAY: February 18

BEST FEATURE: Heart-shaped markings

FAVORITE FOOD: Ice cream (triple scoop)

FAVORITE COLORS: Pink, mint, purple

HOBBIES: Visiting other planets & making friends

ATTRIBUTES: They're aliens

How to Tell If Your Cat Is an Alien

Demands your resources

Studies your behavior

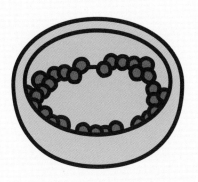

Leaves mysterious signs

Disappears at will

"Take Us to Your Feeder"

6 Reasons to Consider Being an Alien

1. Travel in style

2. Broaden your horizons

3. Make new friends

4. Communicate well

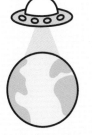

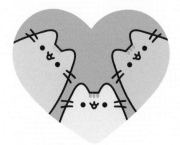

5. Invade Earth

6. Invade hearts

Pastel Pusheens' Favorite Things

Ice cream

Popsicles

Marshmallows

Each other

Pastel Pusheens' Guide to Earthling Artifacts

"Snuggle cube"

"Food magnet"

"Fluff extractor"

"Squiggle friend"

Anatomy of an Alien

Large eyes

Front tentacles

Teleportation mark

Back tentacle

How to Make
First Contact

Prepare a landing pad

Send out a signal

Wait for their arrival

Make a peace offering

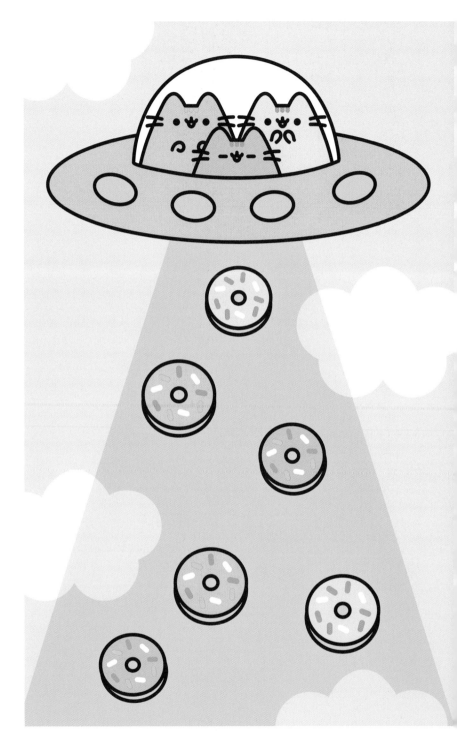

Snacks for Aliens

UF⊙s

Star fruit

~~Human beans~~

Pastel Pusheen

Pastel

Cute

Friendly

Uplifting

Dragonsheen

GENDER: Girl

BIRTHDAY: February 18

BEST FEATURE: Dangerous breath

FAVORITE FOOD: Toasted marshmallows

FAVORITE COLOR: Gold

HOBBIES: Breathing fire & collecting things

ATTRIBUTES: Warm & cuddly

Your Cat May Be a Dragon If . . .

They hoard treasure

They perch on high

They have dangerous breath!

Types of Dragon Breath

Fire

Ice

Electricity

Hair

The Life Cycle
of Dragons

Egg

Hatchling

Young adult

Big bub

Ways to Defend Against Dragons

Build a fort

Distract with shiny stuff

Toss a ball

Give tummy rubs

I'M BUSY

DRAGON FRIENDS

DRAGON BO

DRAGON SLOTH

DRAGON CHEEK

DRAGON STORMY

DRAGON PIP

Treasures Worth Keeping

Gold

Gems

Friends

Warm & cuddly

Staying Warm with Dragonsheen

Light a cozy fire

Make fresh popcorn

Wrap up in blankets

Take a hot bath

Dragonsheen's BBQ Techniques

Indirect cooking

Direct cooking

Smoking

Resting

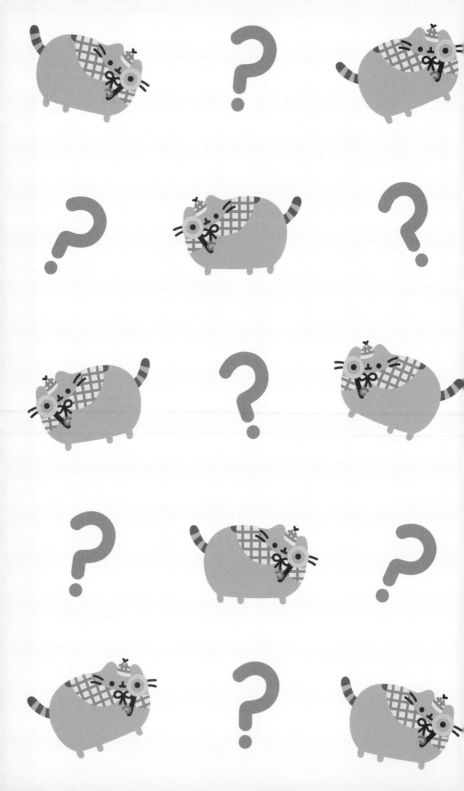

Detective Pusheen

GENDER: Girl

BIRTHDAY: February 18

BEST FEATURE: Her smarts

FAVORITE FOOD: Cookies

FAVORITE COLOR: Caramel

HOBBIES: Reading & solving mysteries

ATTRIBUTES: Intelligent & hardworking

The Mystery of the Hairy Sofa

Arrive at the scene

Gather the evidence

[UNSOLVED]

Detective Pusheen:
The Mystery of the Lost Sock

Examine the scene

Review the facts

Look for clues

Tail your suspect

Case closed

Solving the Mystery:
Who Ate the Cookie?

Solving the Mystery:
A Cupboard

1. Wait for an opening

2. Enter the cupboard

3. It is dark!

4. Become frightened

5. Exit the cupboard

6. To be continued

Purrlock Holmes

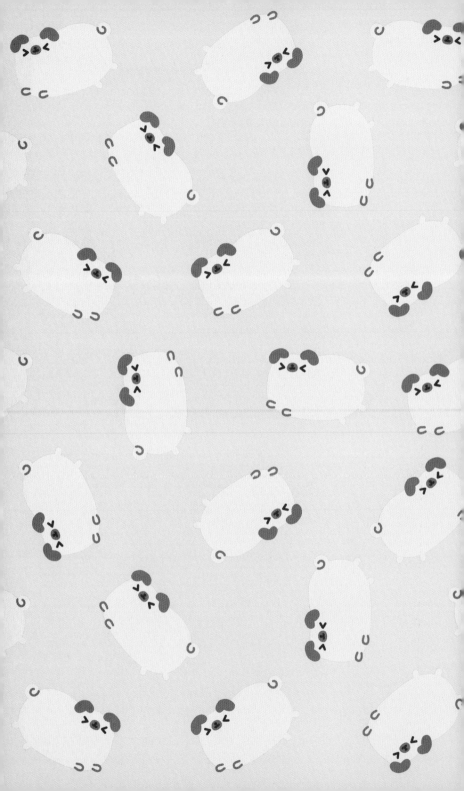

Pugsheen

GENDER: Girl

BIRTHDAY: February 18

BEST FEATURE: Cinnamon bun tail

FAVORITE FOOD: All of them

FAVORITE COLOR: Yellow

HOBBIES: Playing & going for walks

ATTRIBUTES: Sweet, curious, lazy

Places That Dogs Belong

The toilet: no

Your shoes: no

The table: no

Your bag: no

This thing: ???

Your heart: yes

How to Achieve Your Goals

Set your goal

Be flexible

Have patience

Success!

6 REASONS
You Should Consider Being a Dog

1. Free food

2. Free rent

3. Sleep as long
as you want to

4. Look great
with no effort

5. Toes look
like beans

6. Positive
outlook

Naptime

Places I Sat Yesterday

7 a.m.: a door

12 p.m.: a door

7 p.m.: a table

10 p.m.: a people

Acknowledgments

I would like to sincerely thank the following people who helped make this book a reality.

First to the Pusheen creative team, whose wonderful teamwork made this endeavor (and all things Pusheen) possible:

Jess Anca	Jing Ouyang
Katie Belton	Kristin Ridgley
Hayley Gallat	Jessica Rusher
Alyson Kayne	Shane Swinnea
Heather McKenna	Jessi Zabarsky

Thanks as well to our phenomenal director of project management, Cassandra Lipin, and director of licensing, Cate D'Allessandro, whose organizational and coordination skills have been invaluable.

I would also like to thank:

My partner and Pusheen cofounder, Andrew Duff, for being my best friend and a constant source of love, support, and punny jokes.

My literary agent, Myrsini Stephanides, for all of her support, enthusiasm, and cute cat photos.

My editors at Simon & Schuster, Lauren Spiegel and Rebecca Strobel, for giving me the opportunity to publish this book, and for always supporting and believing in Pusheen.

And most importantly, to all the fans who have supported Pusheen over the last decade: Thank you so much!

For More Pusheen, Find Her Online

www.pusheen.com

Instagram: @pusheen

Facebook: @pusheen

Twitter: @pusheen

www.youtube.com/pusheenthecat